THE LONGEST TOTAL

SOLAR ECLIPSE

OF THE CENTURY

July 20, 2009 – July 20, 2010

CATHERINE MENG

SplitLevel Texts
Ann Arbor, MI 48103
http://www.splitleveltexts.com

Copyright © 2013 by Catherine Meng
Cover design by Melissa Dettloff
Cover illustration by Melissa Dettloff

Thanks to MICHIGAN PUBLISHING for
assistance in our publishing efforts

ISBN: 978-0-9858111-3-6
Library of Congress Control Number: 2013937712
Printed in the United States of America

THE LONGEST TOTAL
SOLAR ECLIPSE
OF THE CENTURY

for Alice Panther

You should quit drinking. You should go to the dentist. You should make a dentist appointment. You should learn Spanish. You should throw the ball for the dog. You should call your mother. No, you should buy a new battery for your phone, then call your mother. You should stop talking to yourself. You should stop scratching. You should walk to work. You should go to bed. You should brush your teeth. You should write a poem. You should lock up your bike. You should set the alarm. You should save this document. You should title this document. You should document lots of things you don't. You should take out the recycling. You should get that print framed. You should drink more water. You should smoke a cigarette. You should quit smoking. You should go to bed. You should wash your face. You should floss your teeth more. You should finish reading the Maximus poems. You should go to bed. You should wake up early. You should get married. You should have a baby. You should eat more raw vegetables. You should check that out. I'll send you the link.

Spring is always in the past.
> —Leslie Scalapino

> *Myth is the centrifugal suction pulling
centers apart into other circles, new centers, rings, circles within circles
expanding and contracting...*
> —Jed Rasula

*But
I forget. What's my plot?*
> —Alice Notley

THE LONGEST TOTAL SOLAR ECLIPSE
OF THE CENTURY

The next event from this series will be on August 2, 2027
—Wikipedia

Coughed into the untoward –
a sundered social hour
of institutional coffee served in cups
California has deemed illegal
          but has a surplus to use up. Uncertain

whose face   it is correct   to now
spew into.
Whose sandwich to spit.
Whose pop art to suck.

A meander.

A silver spoon in the wrong end of July.

A troubling pleasure
where jasmine esters rub
through fumes of dumpster

where rats nest
in ivy splay
& pigeons roost
          shitting all day on the same row of cars.

At the gate
          traffic pushes toward the city

& the city pushes back.

How the construction of a bridge defines the middle distance. How the
construction of metaphor

defines the third dimension –

the lines themselves
colluding with depth.

How they seem not at all
                but a meander.

Or a dinner
or a dinner party
or a party by itself blankly picking its nose.

This thing you do to be entertained.

A drive & a greet & a talk & an eat
the expectation
of how the remains of the scene
choose to repeat & repeat

        what the spider's web
calls into question –

how the outer frame is two anchor lines
that join to form
an upside down triangle

                that define the middle distance's depth –

I HAD A BIG DREAM: My car explodes. A crowd gathers.
I pretend it isn't my car
& walk off stage left
gnawing a turnip with my dull teeth.

                                        *

Making sense is for mothers
& the effect is
            collapsible
            where it meets the absurd –

            manners & gill nets & all the obvious jobs asunder

where the measure
swore off the doctor,
wore a top hat to the opera
& woke with enormity

so far from the continent where this event was preparing to take place.

In the poetry of the time
there were beautiful fish on every other line.

In the real world (the one I lodged between

there were petitions
about them
                    but no real fish.

What was left was the center
preparing to give. A weak spot

where it yawns in (glaciers who crush their attendants
a soft crumble
audible as the face of a statue
slides to its feet.

Now passing over a vast ocean
each wave cap tumbles white beneath it

each insurrection
moves
in the easiest direction
water always moves

spanning even further
the glance is thrown & much obstructed as a task –

In the incongruencies
the last remainders
of an exploded star wash up

             all torn apart & strung about
as if caught by a cat & flayed –

a glisten of liver left (to show its work
on the landing.

*

I HAD A BIG DREAM: I pull a vine from my mouth. It keeps coming
out, longer than imaginable. It piles up on the table before me in loops
of lush green leaves. Slight but numerous. Lime green. The woman
sitting across from me tells me it is the 'African Floating Vine' known
to cause choking, possible death, & to stunt the growth of leg hair.

            I remain shored
among pilings –

            shifting information, walking
from point A to point B
and back again,
cutting food
into other shapes of food,
moving the car
every second Tuesday for street sweeping
on the right side
then moving the car
every second Wednesday for street sweeping
on the left side,
moving the car
when the signs say I should,
washing parts of the body
or the whole thing, washing coffee cups
& knives, getting everything clean enough
to get everything dirty again.

At my bad's deadside I seen it was steaming.

The warm comes without sound.

But I want to see
                    the wicked stitch
where the two extremes flow toward solution.
The sandwich
invented to facilitate simultaneous
eating & gambling.

I've moved around the parts
but it doesn't hold up against what I've been told –

unhinged from its own gradations
totality occurs
where it caves

as the path narrows,
          a card house exhales in on itself–
as the face of the statue
slides to its feet.

The middle is its own extreme.

Proving what?
I fill in my own gap.

MANNERISM

...the familiar figure in an unfamiliar setting surrounded by unseen, but felt, quotation marks. – Wikipedia

The human form is a stand-in (reaction
that distorts point of view.
Pure gesture. Pure motion.

Emotion is rendered as background
where plastic bags get caught
in the upper cross-hatchings
or soggily
clog drains.

Still, you rise cleated
with the round shapes
of only one sun
to find yourself

in the middle of a diorama
passing through Phoenix

where the dew cannot climb
where deep lakes are reputed to be
where someone saw a golden eagle

where cracks in the cement-siding
map what the struts know
lines on the face where a frown wants to go

& the town is a cloud-dump
& it is warm when it shouldn't be.

BYCATCH

It is impossible just starting out not to be self-centered.
But let us proceed to the loss of independence –

We are in a book where nail polish has left crimson skids
on the pages
                              read once before & tradition
                                        keeps tempo
                                        with a circular saw.

Where the GPS drops out
                the map appears to curl in on itself
then reverse curve.

The land mass close but never fully approached –

What had been silent
          now   expels a low dirge –

but we can not curl it correctly
the center keeps slipping –
spiraling out the way a tendril must
                    express its own gravity

where we keep confusing our coffee cups
made blind
by such amorous sun.

This represents what has been done before.
A showy excursion into the already said.

                                 All the B-sides waiting to be discovered
as worthy. Multi-tasking
to the tune of distraction

      how wheat smells when it sprouts its first tillers as if it knows
      of its own demise so why not

find a note & hold it to the nose of the world
just before the stock market opens
with the clang of a bell
      & the threshers arrive with their scythes.

MUSICAL CHAIRS

Among the buildings at the center
            arrested by their own shadows

one hears a little of what one wants to.

We have to show our work to find where we are in the equation –

Impossible to recall
the world before
the structure exposed
its dependence on myth

before time moved forward by stating it did.

        No hashing algorithm, no matter how clever, can avoid these
collisions.

The background drips
into the faces. The faces
are always the same;

difficult to separate the diagram
that surrounds them
from the one that they create.

Where you write in the margin
look up
if you don't know the meaning.

On the Anniversary of Our Spinning

I was in Paris on the Ferris wheel with Tom when the planes hit. We
didn't speak French. On the streets meandering back to the broke-
down hotel, it was obvious by the way people walked & the faces they
displayed something had changed. It was 2 hours before anyone told
us. We hung like sleepy spiders in a bubble.

We didn't speak French but sirens sounded the same. People wept
while reading their email at internet cafes. A man, surfacing from
the Metro stopped us & asked if we were American, then told us in
a thick French accent, America got what it deserved. We hung like
sleepy spiders in a bubble. Overnight the trashcans disappeared &
were replaced with clear plastic bags hung on metal frames. I started
smoking again for the first time since my father had died that spring.

Our return flight on September 12 was cancelled. People wept while
reading their email at internet cafes. We spent the next 6 days on
over-draft protection, drinking 3-franc bottles of wine and walking
the length of Paris: north to south, south to north, east to west, west
to east then north to south again. We saw a monkey masturbating
at the Ménagerie du Jardin des Plantes. The Luxembourg gardens
were deserted. We found every bar with its TV tuned to a newscast
in English. After day 5 only 1 remained. My step-mother emailed
saying, there are worse places to be stuck. A woman crumpled at the
computer beside me. We hung like sleepy spiders in a bubble.

When the Charles de Gaulle airport opened again we waited in a
snaking line for 6 hours pushing our suitcases forward with our feet.
The ticket agent said, you're American, no? We said, yes. She said,
you're in First Class, no? We said, no. She said, you're in First Class.
We said, no. She said, you're in First Class and handed us tickets that
said we were in First Class. They showed Moulin Rouge! on the plane
& served us a 4-course meal with wine pairings, real silverware, and
cloth napkins. We were surprised how well Nicole Kidman could sing.
I cried for the first time since my father had died that spring.

The next day I returned to my job where I was paid 8 dollars an hour
to walk people to their table & pull out their chairs and say, enjoy
your dinner with a smile. People talked & cried & drank too much &
looked up into the sky more often. The ravaged web was everywhere.
There was no sense it would ever be re-spun.

MUSICAL CHAIRS

This is the language seen
in the leafless winter passing –

sounding out 'one's self'

is the story beginning
the same way it ends –

pushing toward the front of the city & the city pushing back.

     The thought as it over takes veins
dropping into the moment
when the music stops

is what we build the self around –

an intrinsic confidence in the riddle's solution
                    (harp accompaniment at points of emotional stress
appearing
disappearing –

                              between the trees
                              the sun reflected
                              from a reputed lake.

<u>On foot</u>

I traverse the city twice a day passing the hospital & its tide pools of
smoking nurses, jammy-faced kids in strollers pushed by Guatemalan
nannies, painting crews clung like spiders to houses, playgrounds of
sand-eating, gardeners elbow-deep in manure, posters for missing cats
& children, the Hare Krishna temple & the bereft Hare
loitering under a cherry tree
that muddles the sidewalk
with its sticky maroon
of dropped fruit.

<u>MUSICAL CHAIRS</u>

Moving at a good clip
then stopped in my tracks
by this regenerate need for relief –

I know nothing of these words

                        until they cross the scalp & make
contact with my teeth.

I reverse his layout to reflect this opposite shore.
Long & white are my fingers, as the ninth wave of the sea.

And it is true here, as it was there
part of the flower of this work   is a horrible smell.

<u>RE: Reading</u>

My first love is a beech tree I climb, age 8. There is one set of branches
that are a table & chair where I sit & eat imaginary meals with my
imaginary family. Higher up is 'the sitting room in the attic' with an
easy chair, side table, & a foot rest. The leaves

are slight but numerous. Lime green. In summer, I am completely
enclosed. Cloaked. Inside & above the scene. In winter, when its limbs
are bare, I can see into all the snow choked yards surrounding & jump

directly from half-way up into an impossibly deep drift. Other low
branches covered with ice I slide down, into a space near the base
of the trunk that opens like a silent white amphitheater I call 'the
cathedral'. So why am I surprised to read this morning: 'Beech' is a
common synonym for 'literature'?

<u>MUSICAL CHAIRS</u>

The last stretch leads to another last stretch
all the way to the end
where one chair is left

in which the last player sits

tapping his foot to the scratch in the lock groove.
When I come across this marginalia
later I follow
my former-self's directive & look up

to see the shadow of the world
edging out the moon.

OFF-SEASON

The rising moon
rising beyond a stand of birches
makes them closer
closer than the classic-rock angels of yore

until it is no longer easy to differentiate

the primary swell
from the secondary swell
from the tertiary swell

until it is no longer easy
to balance an egg on its point.

One last locust falls without
fanfare. Star-clusters cough & sizzle.

Watermelons are sold from a truck
in the wedge weeds along some frontage road.

This was the September
the economy became a character

pitied as often vibrancy is.

But I, a hack
dead to the shine,

cross as easily as dust
between the two extremes within a season,

plucking out
the many eyes

in the bank's lobby

where the tiles divide equally
around a ridiculous fountain

gone dry.

In the off-season
fishermen teach classes to surfers
on how to read waves.

In the off-season
I didn't feel lousy, exactly –
I just liked the word

followed by a comma
followed by exactly
followed by a dash

M, TU, W, TH, F

Easily influenced, I restrict my exposure, but soon bore & let all the
riff-raff come rushing in. Learning to want impossible things is a sort
of freedom worms & crocodiles don't know. When he said he saw an
eagle I asked if he felt patriotic and he said, it wasn't that kind of eagle.

How the older I get, every car I see could possibly belong to someone I
know. How frequently now, I see a car & assume it is the car owned by
someone I know who drives the same model car. How frequently now,
I am correct in my assumption (the older I get) & how frequently now,
it is an impossible assumption because the person has moved away, has
traded up, or is dead. How the older I get, I am right & wrong more often.

The sound of the nib on the page rekindles early memories of gaining
audible pleasure from film (the quill scribbling on the parchment
followed by a dash of blotting sand. And also men's dress shoes walking
in a parking garage. Wanting to hear those things first hand, then
realizing all the men in parking garages these days wear sneakers.

Passing the same bereft Hare Krishna breaking down cardboard boxes
by the dumpster. Thinking you stole the idea, then realizing there is
only one idea & an infinity of refashions. Everything pathetic & tender
at once. This was a 'roll book' I thought of as a 'role book' where I
assigned myself all the roles. Where I still carry the one in my mind
when I multiply. Absent-mindedly putting the kettle in the refrigerator
three mornings in a row.

I wake earlier & earlier but still end up running to work. Wanting
to photograph this one scrawl of graffiti I've been passing for weeks.
Finally stopping to touch a rock I assumed to be fake to find its
surface solidly cold all the way through. To be that easily shocked. To
look up. To say to one's self: this is real. Wanting to touch everything
now: the barista's smile, the impossible cake, the change in weather,
us, you, whomever you are, reading this, me, twenty years, months,
days, hours from now –

ZEITGEBERS

Yahoo! says the weather is three brown leaves & two green leaves
& the rumpled assumptions get blown from the boughs

whittling down what's in store for you

                             while she's vrooming around town
leaving peel outs in the pavement, so you're left

to read the rubber later. Putting stone tablets back together
in the dim light of your headlamp & getting huge parts of it wrong –

so you are trudging through snow now
& might have to eat the dog.

The space where the thought gets in its car & drives away

                 is the same way stanzas break

the same way playing azure every time I get a Z tile
conjures Ella

drifting, dreaming, in this interlude.

The same way a cat is just a cat you pass & now & again it agrees to be
pet.
There's not much to say about it other than that. You pet the cat

& continue on. In future days there will be other cats
you may or may not pet.

Erin said, it must be revelatory
to see the sun rise.   And the image was a wind swept cliff.

But the actual event I never saw. One moment was pitch

& the next time I looked
all the lights I'd turned on
had become wasteful.

[ZEITGEBER (Los Angeles)]

Waking into the many rings like a cat backing out
of its color. A painter would have a field day
trying to mix this umami of smog. I didn't want to

wake the boy. The neighbor waved as if he knew me.
        A scene from a novel I read once where the characters
        were these very same trees.

As for the sky, now the sun was in it. And I was across the street looking
back

from the surface
of an oversized picture window.

[ZEITGEBER]

Day Light Savings Time has ended
so now begins the 'it's really 7 not 6' part of the year.
The clocks righted, my right hand writing
& no rain in sight.

Drought was a subject we didn't speak of.

I surround myself with people that get enough sleep.
Regardless, she arrives in her gold car
at her appointed time & finds me

living in someone else's house,
drinking someone else's coffee
saying obvious things
with the obvious words

in this new sun. I am past hyper & part grizzly.
Shorn clean & dashed through

and & and

drawing the character of the ampersand in the air with my finger

I wake the baby.
I bring exhaustion to this house

& torn down like an empire of free will

I flood these streets
like Bono.

[ZEITGEBER]

I couldn't participate in the bridge trauma. I had a silly, side-winding
under-standing of commute.

              It had to do with the native peoples of Alaska.
That's called clanging.

Everything sounding like a pesky owl that has nothing to do with the
subject
& then we are rowing around, dipping our hands in the water

to feel the cold accentuate the bones in our fingers.

Water
with a dull sun
in the soot of it. Goaded by the graph

the subject becomes flaccid, wearing holes in its cuffs
until thumbs poke out.
We can make tools!
We can kill other things!
We should title this progress.

[ZEITGEBER]

Earlier lit the sky shifts
into a more cautionary gear   slow enough to note
the color & shapes of landmarks, the way they slouch
against the background,
nonchalantly spilling.
                    Subjects reissue themselves with revised introductions.

The asphalt includes 10 new pages of notes.
The sky has an expert wax deftly in light of recent regime changes.
The clouds cut 2 chapters from their original text & add a new section
discussing babysitters.
The moon releases a 4.5 billion year anniversary collector's edition
with many top-notch photographs.
The sun shines like it will never go out of print.
Squirrels are still correcting their galleys.

I have written the first sentence of this
but the rest
is a simmering caldron that smells so strongly of death rags
I don't dare taste it. I just stir it
every few hours to prevent scorching
& when whimsy strikes
I throw in a canoe.

ORCHESTRAL SCHEMATICS

What fraction of the actual is barely a bat ear.
                    The other (professional Catherine
waits in her office for this to be read.

Seattle somewhere behind

the continent laid out to the left

the opening credits of North by Northwest

the jowls of Gregory Peck

other unremarkable lapses

to remark on them all

hydration, defecation, vacation, holidays, phone calls, moles checked,
checks cashed, an un-cashed check moldering under a rock brought back
from New Mexico on my desk, hoses coiled, calls missed, beds unmade,
the unusual, show-stopping properties of a bridge that keeps breaking –

Then the blank insurmountable edge of the continent
                            sheered off quick as a drum fill

& we have a cliff
where our talk gets thrown apart by the wind.

Unable to separate the dread out
once it sets up shop in the sound
                         we float un-tethered toward the third direction
lifted & carried
then caught

by the sticky reverse wail of a lily –

Seattle somewhere behind.
The continent laid out to the left.

I shudder to think what detail was missed.

I mean, I woke to such silence
I thought I'd gone deaf.

GOAT FARMERS OF URUGUAY

A goat farmer grows belligerent in a comment field.
We don't blame him. We spill juice on him. It flows over the tops of
our shirts.
A big drab-smelling no.

This is what we wield so nicely, now that the rain has past

& commas come forward on shy hooves
bending into the intent they were meant for.

An infiltration of ants conquer my desk.

I said, please feel free to contact me but grew annoyed when anyone
did.

Then it was Friday, riding a chariot driven by two cats.
In that way   I was implicated.

Amused fathers compared babies as if posing
for a calendar to raise funds for humans.
Nobody answered the phone
until I did & there was wrath
to be had in my ear. The tigers entered
& that was the end of it. We watched the debris

float around in the ocean somewhere off the coast of Florida.
At first it was weird because they were letting us watch television in

school. Then it was weird because the people on television died
& we were expected to be shocked & sad
but previously we'd been told people on TV weren't real.

Same with the blogs.
        Whatever nascent understanding we'd had about empathy
had its limbs hacked off
        right from the start.

I woke on another planet
where people ate dirt & I thought it seemed strange
I didn't find this strange & my blind acceptance
reminded me of the prologue to the century.

I told them, without using the cue cards: once you put your trust in
statistics and university studies backed by pharmaceutical companies
the brain activity of 10 year-olds & psychopaths look identical

when the subject is asked to imagine green. This resulted in a soaring
approval rating.

The goats were in fast motion. Although I felt bad for the sun
I sided with the moon.
                Go on.   I gave something a little push

& it drifted out over the silver-flashed surface –

a thought we'd all had in the immediate aftermath
                finally setting off for somewhere other   free

to gouge deep irreparable grooves
in the dreary hearts of earthbound men.

GEMINIDS

I couldn't believe   how long the conversation   lasted I couldn't

    believe how many instances of smog

we listed each more nuanced

        until it built
        but was closer   to each particle

trailing off   until there was more space   around the words

            than words   catching up

        with the self   in free fall means   caring less.

    It will come to me.   That's what I say   when I stare into space.

    The space   where the word should be is a creamy brown surface

on which nothing will float.   It is the opposite of the Dead

        Sea but nothing lives there. It is not dichotomy. It exists

& is both   full of stars   burning out.

And then it warmed up. I collided with sloth. The problem arose

& the image is dripping.

                              If this is a poem

it should have two lungs right here. Is there no end to my not getting
it?

Or do I get it so good   I turn it over   & begin again

            & it begins again –

I think this.   Cutting into the breathing chest
                                to find the two lungs –

just seeing them
            makes breathing easier   the two of them

dreaming the same dream   hurtling through space   as we speak.

THE HUNG

The hunter presented a deer heart but told the Queen it was the girl's
heart & she gobbled his untruth with gusto.

She fried it in a skillet with salt & pepper
& relished every bite

       & we look the other way. It's sad really,

all of our burning faces
in the poem & in life –

   even to say so, attracts the gaze like fly paper until our eyes are
stuck in the gunk of it.

To research   just there   how the rain water

     pools & then dries back at the edges

& once absorbed   disappears completely.

That I had been busy at all. Jumping off
the jargon at a no-name stop &
           tooling around/whiling away

the whole afternoon   so its shape
is the perfect egg memory takes

until I'm ready
to be prepared.

Hung on meat hooks.
Hung by the thumbs.

A silent, cavernous bell in its silent, cavernous tower –

CHAD DEAN HAD A BIG DREAM: in which I did a sonnet's worth of
hanging

until there was no differentiation
because they know not what disturbs them

& here, I mean the hung.Theeeeeeeeeee huuuuuuuuuuuuuuunnnnng.
Theeeeeeeee
huuuuuuuuuunnnnnnngg. Theeeeeeee huuuuuuuuuuunnnnnnnggggg.
Theeeee huuuuuuuunnnnnnnggg. The hung. The hung. The hung the
hung the hung

the hung. And it was church
from that point on.

You must open the eyes of the palms.
To open the eyes of the palms

you must grow in the eyes of the rain. To forget
the geese of this & then remember

they are also made of eyes.
That I would out myself like that

before the seething congregation   & what do they know
of my debt?

The hung. Theeeeeeee huuuuuunnnnngggg. The
hung the hung the hungthehungthehungthehungthehung. Theeeeeee
huuuuuunnnng. Theeeeeeeeee
hung.

This algorithm gains access to my spasm.
         A wee pot of tea   I told myself   was all I needed.

I said, sorry for the inconvenience
when the eyes refused to be deleted.

         To take back my speech
we must tease forth the nuance.

The hung had a beat. I'm sure of it.
And the beat was served to the audience

              & they swallowed it whole.

The method is moot. Whatever the meaning. The message
is seasoned, sautéed, & eaten.
         Now the hung were in ALL-CAPS

& the ALL-CAPS sprung eyes.

ESCAPE FROM THE LANGUAGE LAB

*The supreme artifice comes in the Maniera painter's love of deliberately
mis-appropriating a quotation.* -Wikipedia

When we can't wake up we say the coffee is broken
swearing off the master font.
These are not the times of new romans they are
the times of getting blotto on Seinfeld
while frigates
bomb the yonder –

      Sun-dialed by my five o'clock shadow
explicitness fogs the radar
when my mouth gets too close
            we are nowhere
tra-la-lalling, spurred on
by false erasures
the kind where you float out
beyond the sustain
      until the mind is pure retina
      until there are no myths left to pin this on.

An asterisk stands in for the dream
where we carpool to the third dimension.
To be a fugitive where distortion makes sense
& a shopping mall
is named after Walt Whitman.

        Watching trains couple & de-couple in the train yard
    to tilt your head
to connote you really know what you are seeing.

Cast-off electronics
& old refrigerators leak freon
beneath the heap of park
          named after César Chávez
that was once the city dump
where dogs
can be walked off-leash.
This is always followed
by lapping bowls of water,
curling up on cool cement, &
panting in the shade.

And the reader is always depicted possessing
queerly elongated limbs,
a small head,
& stylized facial features
          while their pose
seems difficult
or contrived
against a flat background
of indeterminate dimensions.

To wield nothing other than a stance.
To stand that way for centuries.

          That's how long it takes   to think

one clear thought through to its multiple ends.

That your real silk tie is a red heart.
That your red silk tie is a real heart.
That the bell is where the ring is housed.
That the rains came   and washed the spider out

  & in the space
where Walden once stood

is a replica of the house
with bars on the windows *&* door
so you can peer in on the table, the chair,
the potbelly stove.

ALTERNATOR, ALSO KNOWN AS LUNAR CAUSTIC, OCCURING IN THE INTERSTICES, AND MY TRIP TO THE SAN FRANCISCO ACADEMY OF SCIENCE

The wormhole itself is two copies of the black hole geometry connected by a throat – the throat, or passageway, is called an Einstein-Rosen bridge.
–NASA website

Among this multi-pronged mission
among these points I've made: my corporate corner store, my
absenteeism, the spider
spinning its own grave

I elect the hysteria of neon pink & its self-made dream –

       I got on well with the better season
            when you are allowed to read fifty books in one month.

It was writing two poems at once
the engine & the alternator
slapping each other's asses in the lapses.

       Powerless against its outward reaching
       my sestina went rogue.
       This is not that sestina.

And the house was stately with warmth.
And the subject is the muse is the sestina:
a century plant I pass
on my way to & from work.

I submit my theory & my theory submits to whatever whimsy I choose
to locate in the spoiled milk.

[PRESS RECORD]

We drove across the Bay Bridge
& into the city. The light was particular.
You said my camera was the golden mean
I said lunar caustic

while we follow the toddler
toddling around
the parents locate each other
using their cell phones like walkie-talkies
in the humid blub of the aquarium nethers

below the water now in a tunnel of glass
a turtle rests its creamy belly just above our heads
& I realize I am hot in my wool.

I touch the sea urchin in the tide pool exhibit
with two fingers
as I am told.

And what does it feel like?
Spikes made soft
by the distortion of depth.

When certain things get in order
certain other things disorder.
                I chloroformed my sestina
                & now we're back on track.

I become curious again about making it obvious. How the ash drifts

& lands   clear across town

in the dog's water dish.

I cross a large body of water
to place myself in a tube
          not connecting two things, but preserved
by itself, as a fragment, beneath the waters.

                    Meanwhile, the sestina crossed through the page
                    & assaulted the reader, the writer. Same diff.

How the action run through the device
is demystified –

this is about demystifying the action
occurring in the interstices
                    how the sestina skulks
                    and won't make eye contact.
                    This is not that sestina.

Is it just me, or are these clouds from the 19th century?
So formal   so romantic
an egg cup & then a teaspoon tap

to crack the shell
the sound –
just look at the bridge struts

the slant response in close proximity
to what?

A picture postcard we row through –
the expanse before it was conquered,
shot through with such unearthly slats of light.

On the banks of the gate
somewhere beneath the cloak

such light reacts the silver nitrate
& the scene is as it always is
                    with listlessness for a metronome

slow cars
moving in rows

the obstacle
the traversed
a fold or a pleat
the permeable mind
the interstices

made soft by the perception of depth.

    Same way cream is so nice in your coffee after not having it for
awhile.

I'll leave you with that. So you have something to sup.
Go & be studious in the plush placebo of rainfall!
And return to us in the spring
with the sun in your eyeballs, your mustache well oiled

& read to us
the riot act
as told to you by the trees.

I quip to myself   cut myself out

I quip 'cut it out' in quotes
put a tail on my q

to connote it is not a g. To understand later what it is I wrote –

        Something about the complex lives
of lowercase letters.
                Now back to that sestina I've been meaning to write.

The envoy went something like this:
There were synchronicities in my in-box that Valentine's Day –
yesterday – too stark to explain

as synchronicities & valentines often are

they just exist
for us to gape at.   I always think of the Grand Canyon
when I write the word 'gape' –
                        the roaring expanse
before a bridge exists.

    My sestina caught a flat. So now it has one of those donut tires & its
hazards flashing & crawls
slow as a crab just after it molts. This is not that sestina. But also it is.

There was a sign that said not to take pictures
of the octopus because it was frightened by the flash.

THE CENTURY PLANT

Suckers, my suckers ring round in lapses
& my interstices convey spider
geometry in the whine of a century
where a riddled spike lies in wait at the core.
Tethered, as undertow does to the waves
I climb beyond the surface conceit

& deranged by the neon made neat
mouth off inside the border's collapse
that defines the border of the prior grave.
As each margin's own spine
unfurls in the wake of the self before
the dead hum a bit, drained by this conjury

throttled from the wizen rosette to stand sentry
against academy, where the deleted
constellations known in seafaring lore
are irrational constants on a map
that crashes fat the sky
until the literal disaster is one harbor wave.

Such translations deny what rises from this page.
You reader, may be moved to perjury
& you hearer, may try to side with the spider –
but taking sides is a cop out. A poem may be sweet
but it is not kind. We are not holding hands. I lapse
& then mine the dead for ore

until I am fucking the last remaining metaphor
thrust into the shuddering wave after wave
my cyme blooming yellow buds, one for each gasp
connected by a century
put in motion long before this concrete
was mixed, placed, leveled, and dried.

In my future, even as I die
my suckers echo to before
the first sucker thought it wise to repeat
& the moon driven waves
slide & sluice toward another century
surrounded by its own collapse –

forever spiraling from the source craving
each simultaneous formed & ruined history –
until the beat synchs up to the self it overlaps.

AT IMPEDMENT

This Fat Tuesday began with a marching band & ended supping soup
over discussions too troublesome to incorporate into the tuba bleat. Elliot
blamed the juxtaposition of bird song & starving to death. But I found
a stark accuracy there, corresponding with my feelings towards spring.

February 16, 2010

I write letters to Deborah & tell her about the problems I'm having with
writing, but by the 6th page, when my hand starts cramping & I grow
weary from my own complaining, I protest I'm not depressed. It is always
the same pattern: my difficultly followed by a self-correction, a self I
reveal to myself that is more willing than the self I was in the first few
pages to keep on doing what it is I'm doing. I'm always of two minds.
The letters display the two minds at once. Deborah is a Texan but lives
in Argentina now & writes me letters on pink stationary with pictures
drawn in the margins of plants & long descriptions of the cafes she writes
me from where the coffee is served with chocolate bars you stir into your
coffee so it melts. She has just had a baby, so her letters now are full of
her own surprises. To hear a mother describe nursing for the first time
is so fantastic. I could listen to mothers talking about nursing for the
first time for a long while.

February 24, 2010

Elliot's father has been dying for a long while. But now he is REALLY dying. In a phone call, the endless act of dying catches up to the present. My body displays the familiar traits of shock – like electricity gone down the wrong tube. I change the song playing on my headphones six times before I look up from the same device where the call had come and there are children playing in the school yard I am walking past. Divided in small clots as children playing do – but always two – off to the side – away from the larger groups – pressing themselves up against the chain link fence, their limbs twine together in whispers of a game I'm sure I've played but have forgotten all the rules to.

I don't covet this. I don't covet that. I exist outside a smallness.

I HAD A BIG DREAM: I forgot I was house-sitting for Jenya's parents & by the time I remembered, already a week into their absence, their house had been ransacked & robbed. They had left me a plate of brownies already gone stale & a note that said, make yourself at home.

I woke drenched in sweat but I wrote: I work dressed in sweat.

February 26, 2010

I am trying to synch up the mind/body problem with the Berkeley/ Oakland problem and it is going tenuous at best. Elliot suggests I overlay the human spine in utero on a map of the Bay Area, but that would make Mill Valley or San Francisco the head depending on which way is up, and Berkeley and Oakland the stomach the guts the ass. The delta as a fluid around, breathing in & out. Meanwhile a sonnet I've been trying to write has the shape of many pathetic dust devils trying to start up but then dropping out mid-devil. Jared asked what I'm writing about and I deflected. As I write this, I can hear my landlord, whistling the first bars of Pomp & Circumstance over & over again. So the graduation never fully starts or ends.

Farewell the neighing steed and the shrill trump
The spirit-stirring drum, th'ear-piercing fife,
The royal banner, and all quality,
Pride, pomp, and circumstance of glorious war!

February 27, 2010

I fell asleep during my third viewing of Raging Bull. I said I'd had some small breakthroughs.

February 28, 2010

At Carl's bedside we talk about the protests at Berkeley, the Symbionese Liberation Army, the winter Olympics, Raging Bull, and Roman Polanski. We agree there is no unified voice. Carl's breathing lapses every 25 breaths into apnea. Glenn Gould trounces across the keys. The hospice nurse says, now you just wait, followed by, it's much like a birth.

Elliot & I walk to a nearby bodega to get coffee. But there is no coffee so a fresh pot is made. While we wait, I film a video with my phone of the slushy machines twirling. It is 10 seconds long & boring. The shop keeper wants to know why I make this video? I can't locate a sensible answer. He asks, do you put it on a website or Facebook? I say, no & no & think I might be lying. I say, I like videos of boring things. I say, I like to watch time passing.

I drive to the airport to pick-up Aunt Shu & get 'lost'. I was directed to
take Rt. 4. Rt. 4 goes east or west & I pick west & drive far into darkness
& sense I'm going the wrong way because none of the landmarks are
there, but at the same time think that it must be the right way
because I am going west –

& west from "here" means Oakland where the airport is. The freeway is
relatively empty & curves & crests through a darkened landscape I can
not see & yet I trust my direction for the first time in many months. I
pass through cities I've never passed through: Crockett, Hercules, Pinole.
I'm unsure how much time has passed. It seems like too long to not be
nervous that I'm lost, but I'm not nervous so it seems like it can't be too
long. Then signs for Oakland & the bay is on my right.

Carl's color has gone ashen. Everyone thinks they should sleep but is
worried he'll die if they do.

March 1, 2010

Cherry blossoms let loose by the rain spangle all the city sidewalks &
continue to loosen   as if the air itself is shedding.

March 2, 2010

[LAPSE]

March 3, 2010

It took twenty years to see a tree is not a tree
and twenty more to say it is a tree

March 4, 2010

THE WOODPECKER

One leg of the dock is carried off
by an unprecedented tide

free-standing now, each syllable
pronounces the darkness's edge –

to stanch the grief of one image
is to create another in close proximity

to convey Matterhorn, as it is now
confined to the lines of this poem

to crawl into the shape of the word as a wolf would
& wear the lucky pants & the four steep faces.

This is an example of how
trepidation becomes a verb

how fluid becomes rock
& also a tourist attraction

[the mountain loves me this I know,
because the Wikipedia entry told me so]

the last peak to be conquered
marks the end of the golden age of alpinism

and The Field Guide to Poetry
said nothing would grow in this type of soil.

No matter. The present concocts its own event.
Not wakefulness –

but the tinny whistle's tinny sheen
same way a figure is ascribed to inspiration

or not wanting to finish the book
because it's too good. Dare I say anything

for fear it will dismantle the raw stump of cognition
yet pieces unsaid still cloy on the tongue

& hinge apart the forever gears, the tender gills
we watch so closely

to wring from the space held by the "w" a different meaning
otherwise there will be bells that double-up & toll

coaxed by what? A faint trill in the sunk notion
where dawn climbs 14 over-wrought lines to some other door

invited by the stucco's contour
brought forth by voices arriving

first in the air & then in the ear, a chitter
among treetops

the palpable mote carved between doggerel
& sentiment. There was a bird, or two, on nearly every branch.

How a flock is the sum of all parts. How a flock has
an uncanny resemblance to the days that make up a month

made moot by a more forceful lapse, that other season –
the arrival of breath, then no breath at all.

You heeded the stop sign
although the street was named Haste & dead ends

at the venn diagram that diagrams your life's work
where 3 circles converge, as your fingers grow bluer

in the purple part where library & archive & apnea overlap
memory disturbs its own fickle tide. These were cues. Not cries.

Yet inseparable, as in the darkness or desert
where suburbs are all one tumble of cool swath continuously

before the advent of hedges
demarcates where your life ends & the Jones' begin

the arrival of woodpecker
depicts something more fragile

a discernible shape to the sound of this weather –
not in like a lion & out like a lamb. But a cavity

for catching rhythm.

DAYLIGHT SAVINGS TIME BEGINS

Sore from reading old words   fashioned to look

like harmony or smell
like mustard gas
                        the eyes fashion the ring

from the shape of a bell –

how it is hard to stay   in this predictable cadence of
grocery & grocery list

to pull the sheets over your head

            & say, grainery   grainery –

*Grainery, it turns out, is not in the free Merriam-Webster Online
Dictionary, where you just searched.*

*However, it is available in our premium Merriam-Webster
Unabridged Dictionary. To see that definition in the Unabridged
Dictionary, start your free trial now.*

If I were to wish for something   wholly unabridged

I wouldn't know what to call it.
                        But it would be

like one of those mythical, hybrid creatures

with the body of a cactus & the talons of a crow

    & three heads: one of the prairie, the other the ocean,

and the last, the moon.

      It would contain many white-washed rooms

soaked by just as many suns
that shined

    by singing
    where the eyes divide exponentially

as seamless as water sluices.

But isn't that what it is like, right at this moment (2pm March 14, 2010

when you press your face
into the air –

when the wind died   it grew.

    There were more details but that was the gist of it.

Basic as crocus is
the gist

& the hive stirring is

the repurposed rift
between the clock & the hour.

The mind/body connection

is also a problem
full of words
we'd be better off

            not saying.

        Torn from
or robbed of

            the self outside the great altruism

of the living breathing   spasm.

To think of tide pools as   separate entities

only at low tide

where the edges have been struck
into a craggy shapeliness

the edges of what?

My person, this Catherine
this slip of air
        I encumber with the jocular multitasking
        of these shopworn words.

[LAPSE]

Looking for consultation in every slip of light
there is time to stand in

                the sound moving against itself

is cherry blossoms
dismantled by a wind
     as if the air itself is shedding

as if the sleight of hand
is violence

    looking for the missing hour   that came back

in the form of a cat
your mother fed sardines

     just as we unplugged the clock

& after weeks of bereftly gazing to the space where it had been
   we plug it back in.

Days become their own separate entities
precise as a Buddha
     carved from one solid piece of wood

but at the same time sodden
with the thing that went missing –

    the surrounding trunk still ringing
    the space where it once was –

    in the wider eruption

    gauzy colors get scooped
by the shadows
     beyond the smog   it seems

you've been reading
        forever

unfurled even further   each time a revolution completes

& those shadows fall   just as they did

this same time last year   or the one before   or the one before

        so the image overlays the one

we put up some Good Friday the 13th
in preparation for the reckoning –

                        If all your accessories are yellow
                        then you can find them.

        Exercising the oft neglected sets of eyes

that see treason
in the word for trees
                        until those rooms   widen in another version

bumping up against
a future shore   arranged by the incessant

        revisions of the ocean.
                        This
                        always
                        thrumming

        wings beat
        then beat again

        & know your
        family
        from before
        the names
crumbled from the persons
assigned them –

                The sun helps

with the tiny riots the lapses usher in
to forgotten rooms

     covered in bed sheets   seen before in a movie
based on a book most likely
by E.M. Forster.

        While the orator is off in his walled garden
              feeding the koi

you're left spacing out
in the dust motes
        grabbing at handles

of what someone said someone's grandmother said –

[LAPSE]

a swift rainstorm came
with a worry
     the conjury of a hummingbird's impossible nest
then strawberries, then the holiday parable
that began the story:

so they rooooooll back the rock all day on AM radio.   And the sheared-
off bits

that ache in proximity
attempt to fuse in the stutter   between what is & what could have been.

Not regret.   But a stump.   A phantom ventricle

of the muscle   pumping something   to parts that no longer exist.

                                        In like a lion & out like a lion –

yet somehow the nest remains lashed
with only moss & spider web.

A plug
in her own clutch

                        the deftness of her work –
                        the act of staying.
                        As simple as that.

        In retrospect
will now be obvious?

        My owl parts
        turn back on this to see broke crockery, bent frets, & b-flats –

all the roar of the sea in a fungal spore.

                Flashing in through the dapple
the scene depends on being seen.   That it is all one
continuous

eclipse. Eclipsing a prior motive
& then the current motive
is now eclipsed.

CATHERINE MENG FINDS TENSES & PRONOUNS PAINFUL

A shotgun fires & a pair of mourning doves coo up
to the limbs of a Jerusalem olive tree

       [implicate order vs. explicate order]

in relation to entering the desert
& coming out the other side
severed but more fully formed
reflecting back to the reader
the backed out words.

A Adobe Springs Drive turn right
C Cabazone Peak Drive turn left
F Fawn Springs Drive turn right
H Highland Springs Drive turn left
P Poppet Springs Drive turn right

The acrostic my grandmother invented to remember this route was:
Alice Chester Finds Housework Painful.

We all could benefit
from risking temporality
more often
                because I think you'll be happy

to know I saw a bee.
Healthy & engaged

with the magenta lure
of a petunia.

I saw a bee & thought of you somewhere north on a ladder
among the limbs of apple trees.

But in an aside I found out later
a feral cow had been shot & its body dumped
not far from the orchard where you are.
So at that height
if the wind blows right
you are engulfed
in the stench
of flesh rotting.

> I went through airport security
> twice with a lighter in my pocket
> & nothing happened.

The shotgun fires
& people golf.

Twenty years to see a death is not a death
& twenty more to say: it is the anniversary of dying

& twenty more to pin it on the chocolate bunny
whose head I cave in
when my plane was delayed.

The woodpecker's return was it's own event.
Fixing itself
somewhere
to the left of this

plying identity
from each private head

as it is and as it also is a memory

in which to store the future.

I make my own acrostic: Catherine Meng Finds Tenses & Pronouns
Painful

but have yet to find the corresponding streets. And haven't the foggiest
idea of who
I would find or where I would end up if I followed them.

          The quills poke out & pulled further reveal
the full feather
one after another
until we have enough
for a bird wing
where an eye should be.

Until the mind is pure retina
full of songs
older than dirt.

I make my own doctrine and find I am my own triune
the new & collective poems
of three brains
with a time signature

twice removed from the original
roar & whimper
trounced daily

by the commonplace
salt & pepper
the deft duality
between the known
& the said
that rounds smooth
the inner walls

to exist as all three
all at once

the ring of the shot
pins the present
as a constant
in the crosshairs of its sound.

R.I.P. BABY HUMMINGBIRDS

Trevor says, the wave hit & I looked down at my arm & the pain was
abstract.

The headline says, Apples Are The New Fish.

One raven signified something
the human mind resists.

The only shred of evidence is indeed shredded. A few minor clots –

the last remainders of an exploding star.
Hard to spot
unless you're looking –

like a myth
   where it had been

was now a hollow roar.

> *Let a man look for the permanent in the mutable and fleeting; let*
> *him learn to bear the disappearance of things he was wont to*
> *reverence without losing his reverence; let him learn that he is*
> *here, not to work but to be worked on.* – Ralph Waldo Emerson

Three New Yorkers tell me they have recently watched 60 Minutes
& the Bay Bridge is a piece of shit & about to collapse. Three New
Yorkers walk into a bar.

The joke is
a tether
                  tied to
a punch line
             that does not exist.
The Pacific shore is one end of a land soaked with blood.

That the tide thumps in
to wash the other hand.

That I don't know the name of the bird
that ratchets this morning apart with a voice

that sounds like a slight. [Killdeer]

Passing the house where the century plant's cyme had been
blooming
          to find it chopped down

          a missing throttle through space

a phantom landmark that stands for
a sestina (this is not that sestina
a representation that stands for
a thing
that no longer is.

Same way my trip to NYC was summed up by 2 things that didn't
happen there: that Emerson quote I read on the plane somewhere
over Colorado & the demise of the hummingbird chicks
that had hatched the week before I left. Now the filaments

twine in my recall: NYC = dead hummingbirds = Emerson quote

touching back the former narrative traversed
in reverse

from sea to blooded sea.

I'd learned from a PBS special, narrated by Robert Redford, the San
Francisco Bay was one of the largest natural estuaries in the world
that they planned to fill in until 3 women convinced Ronald Regan
not to.

I try to imagine this Bay without those three women.
Only roads & buildings perched on landfill.

Of the 32 largest cities in the world, 22 are located on estuaries. For
example, New York City is located at the orifice of the Hudson River
estuary.

>   America will forever be what it did not become,
>   and Walden will remain its empty house.

A geode full of residuals
where the light tangles & occasionally fizzes up
to the tongue

unabsorbed by the wake
           & muted by the perception of depth

which I mispronounced frequently as 'death'.

           Not a slip
but a lapse becoming
its own invalid gift.

AFTER A LINE FROM SPICER

I wasn't looking
for a magical clockworkman
but magic
AND ALSO a stock boy
who works at Staples
& wears a brace
to protect his back
when he bends
to load paper
on to shelves.

I want to ask him
what percentage
of that paper
will have poems
written on it.

If we consider
the number of poets
swirling around
in this town
and the percentage
who shop at Staples

I'd guess less
than 1% of that paper

is used to write poems.
Less than 1%
is the magic part
I was looking for.

I'd venture to say
many of the poets
swirling around
this town
are always writing poems
but not always
writing them down.
Maybe that was
the magic part
I was looking for.

I'd venture to say
they are shopping for tin foil
I've seen them!
at the Berkeley Bowl

I'd venture to say
they are shopping for duct tape
I've seen them!
at Walgreen's

I'd venture to say
they are waiting in line
I've seen them!
to buy stamps at the post office

I'd venture to say
they are eating together

I've seen them!
in a café

I'd venture to say
they are walking to work
I've seen them!
waiting on the bus
I've seen them!
strolling through the crowds
of Telegraph Avenue
under a bright
red paper parasol
I've seen them!

in the car next to me
I've seen them!
at a red light.

And I'd venture to say
that the poem
is taking its shape
line by line

projected all the while
line by line
on the inner curve
of the skull & the sky

taking the shape
of the hulking bones
of purple irises
that ricochet off
these hills surrounding

& conflate with the
wheat & diesel
taking the shape
of rings expanding
out into the scene –

I reckon there is no way to count
how many poems
are being written right now.

THIS POEM IS IN FOUR PARTS

When the alarm starts sounding I hold it up to your ear still blocked-up with the warm noise of your dreams & say, do you acknowledge this? I myself, still blocked-up with the warm noise so I ask to define which one I'm hearing. Of course there are birds crossing above. I know this one. Crows.

Yesterday, I didn't write it down, but there was a guy flying a remote control plane in the empty lot across the street & one crow was fixated on chasing it off. He squawked & dove aggressively towards it as if to push it from a copse of pine where the rest of the flock perched brooding. The scene was half-way between amusing & moving. Which was dependant on the perceived size of the threat. Both mine & the crow's.

Though the forecast was neither forthright or scholarly a brightness fuzzed at the edges, making a squint where it hitched up to the present as though still warm in my ear, as though there were true voices in it. This was triggered by a film I'd watched. Something about how the light was shot, conflated with the wind that day when there is no other sound but the shape of it.

Often when I'm writing my feet fall asleep as though I've burned off the body & returned to it through thoughts I haven't yet had & become in that instant an open-ended inquiry. Because she said, this next poem is in three parts. All of my poems are in two or three parts. And I thought that was part of the poem.

DOWN IS THE NEW FLAT

*"2010 oil spill" and "BP oil spill" redirect here. For other oil spills in 2010,
see 2010 oil spill (disambiguation). For the 2006 oil spill involving BP, see
Prudhoe Bay oil spill. For the drilling rig and explosion, see Deepwater
Horizon (disambiguation).* -Wikipedia

It was anyone's guess what the black plume suggested. That it was
a message at all.

I've heard it is cumulative
                    (not calmative)

& by the hundredth time this occurs it is a false frontier
we take apart with our memory
                            a slapstick –
like trying to mop up the mess
with a ShamWow is just trying for show.

        Or am I only surface on which the message unwinds?

I want to drill bit the image
back out of my eye socket

until it dithers its own lawn of unrepentant blades –

                    the sighing kind, that make you double-back
like a rainbow in overdrive –

        aghast at your own profusion.

I resist the impulse to add more to the story

with an asterisk   shining like a tiny black star

over the right shoulder of the r in disaster
because the endnote
would never end.

REF: GRAPH 1.1 – WHERE POETRY EXISTS VS. BEING WRITTEN DOWN

Just outside the door, the vocabulary smacks its lips
within earshot of the internal braying.

> There was no way to incorporate this into The Book of Lapses
I said that I was writing
but hadn't written.

Because sometimes when you say you are writing something
it means you are thinking something

> > > & cataloging your thinking

into groups, rows & lists, chapters, diagrams, pie charts & kingdoms.

Even though you are not physically writing it down   it exists

first as a nagging
> > that you won the raffle,

but if it sets anchor
& can be accessed & re-accessed it becomes
an idea with physical traits
> > which is a trip to Peru

even though it doesn't physically exist

> you will go to Peru

the more you believe it, refer to it, reference it

     you must go to Peru
     it is so obvious

the realer it gets

because you won the raffle.

I write this down   as it comes to me
with no idea beforehand of what will be said.

It is a separate project
one I have little say in.

Until the lines blur, the door diminishes, the levels overlap

& the vocabulary passes me this tray of shining fruit.

The vocabulary holds it forth
as I serve myself first –

the vocabulary unfolds its napkin in its lap & leans in
saying, tell me about this book
that you've been writing.

I HAD A BIG DREAM: I was staying in a tall cold house with many
people sharing many tiny rooms. The sounds of doors being closed
& opened frequently & creeping through long dark hallways. Elliot
& I wanted to talk but we were sharing a room with a pesky kid & an
old man. We'd heard there was a roof with a woodstove. We agreed
to meet there in a half hour. When the appointed time arrived I had
to climb a number of rickety exterior ladders up & up in a drizzle of
cold rain. When we'd both arrived at the roof – it was beautiful – there
was no longer any rain but instead a piercingly clear sky with so
many stars. In the dark we could make out two other bodies stretched
out on a blanket. We were nervous we'd interrupted something, but
then they saw us, and they were poets. They said, come join us. I
offered to get more wood for the woodstove but was told there was
more than enough to keep the fire going all night. Then more people
started streaming up the ladders. More poets. We were whispering our
hellos, giddy yet reverent as if in church. We each found ourselves the
slimmest empty patch in which we could lie down, packed close as a
pack of wolves. There was no conversation. We all just lie there in the
warm glow of the fire & stared up into the sky.

May 22, 2010

FUTURE PIE

I never play zipper when I get a Z tile
although I'm hopeful some day I might

I am saddened
that something so slight
is all my hope
is willing to attach to.

     In an azure mood
the Z tile conjures Ella
the Z alone conjures zebra

& by proxy
a herd of zonkey in Crow Canyon
Elliot has been privy to.

The zonkey is a mythical creature
brought to life by cross-breeding

until I can't see the forest through the trees' reality

so there is little to gauge
what appears to be surface

until there is no distinction

until the century happens concurrently

between what is & was & wasn't said

& we are left in the damp warmth
to find we have legs
                    flabby & weak
but legs
that connect to a joint
in our chest
                    also flabby & weak
but a joint in our chest

we press against & find it breathes.

I scour to get nearer
but end up washing clear
through the internal particulars

until all its meaning & double meanings
slosh over the side
in as many colors as the news

followed by the neat-o making of dinner & my hands
bound by the suds.

Equating our future pie with the first bee sighting.

In the waning pre-full moon
we gawk back
at the squawk box
pinning the blame on the texting conductor
not the text,
or the subtext,
or the context,
or the texture.

I told the woman at Lenscrafters
I wanted my sunglasses tinted as dark as Stevie Wonder's.

She paused as if about to break dishes
& said, Stevie Wonder is blind.

GOOGLE MAPS

The song I have invented astonishes the road
bending into a holler where the trees appear

to be astonished –

                                      unwinding
                                      from their shallows & queues

                                      we find grace retired softly
                                      in deft strokes

                                      each blade bent back against
                                      a dark purple-brown

                                      thatched in with the greater qualities
                                      of all the words that rhyme

standing out in the catastrophe, my ghost
this late in the game peels so deeply

it is hard to look at its tender parts exposed –

waves of it, acres of it
felled & erected

exponentially greater than the pixels
that make up the satellite image.

The fake-out rhetoric. The call to arms
we make up as we go along

           making sense or nonsense
           of the white space

           enjambed by the mechanical
           stupefied wander & catch

           the gears in the chest turned
           by the stupefied wandering breath

using street view ten years after your death
to find
your car still parked in your driveway.

MAP QUEST

My landlord tells me, shoot for the stars!

& when he's down on his luck he says, get the rope.
I listen & hear the gears churn open, then mangle & stall.

The weather is more often than not a bully
although the ganglia of one-way streets

make language, for a time, seem useful

I'm not sure if this is relevant to
or crossing through the membrane's edge

where the two muddle at the center,
& I mix up alloy with what a sailor says.

Or the part where you mix up
the sugar with the salt & ruin the tart.

But we eat it anyway
& in four months you are dead.

We are living in the potential bull's eye
of whatever that is.

Because the event is secondary
to the commonplace action

a white-washed prop
holding nothing in place –

Where the sing-song parts
chime for more seed

the lines of cartographers barely waver.
So the way is measured & set –

yet again & again I return
to lose my place

intent upon the beat
of the hand-drawn shoreline
implied by the ocean,

to dis-resemble the event
& refresh my current location.

And of course, OF COURSE
there is a whale in that ocean.

We must believe
without hearing it.

Otherwise, the masterpiece is only
briefly snared

where the shadow's interiors
pronounce the wainscoting

where you startle from sleep
to write down Wyoming

where speed-limit signs
shot through with bullet holes

at the right angle
are shot through with sun.

GAME RESERVE

I try to count out the days of the year
but get caught up in March
which has extra fingers on its hand
so who knows how much time has passed?

I'll keep writing until July & then forever after.

I am sure my vision has gained at least an inch
as I can see now
above the edge of the fence
into a garden overgrown with nasturtium
& populated by cats

washing themselves into statues.

Just because there is no eagle
docsn't mean the eagle isn't here.

Or maybe 'eagle' is really the name for 'crow'.
And the group of them
above me now is saying so. Saying

you dumb fucks! We're eagles!
And the symbol of your country
is a crow.

       As the greengrocer in my mind
is a willful pandering of vainglory
& sinus pressure –

      wrought-iron curlicues
always depict a sylvan scene.

What quill-envy disremembers you,
winged thing? Circling above
without catching
the reference
in the air

between the us of it. The conjured we.

Unobtrusive as sunlight
passing through the bars of the cage
until you've seen it
& an image enters in.

66

– And goaded onward
      through the clot of closely sprung islands
too brief to map

      your subtle wake travels outward
to break against the four surrounding shores.

These are thoughts see

held in by the peripheral desk job
the lunch break brackets
the heat wave's down beat
as the hash marks tumble towards

      the calendric circumference of day after day.

Until the balance shifts
      irreparably into the present
where volumes & verdicts still wait to be read.

I saw nothing new, so I said nothing different. Where it wears a groove

in my synapses
I insert a list of the unaffiliated:

One wood structure
with two in its center.

Things were no longer at play.
It is impossible not
to get caught in the undertow

as if I was the metronome
of what keeps expanding
so all that is left is the widening iambic
just after lightning
& the hairs on your arm
saying I am, I am, I am, and I am too!

But my traces fade just as quickly until
I can't see the point. Only the curled lips before & after
where the roar was

I send to myself as an attachment
& try to make sense of.

When no one is looking

I reach my hand far into the image & pull the tongue
dripping from the bell –

it speaks a malformed echo of what once was its ring & it says:
  you must wear through
  where the clang was
  & catch up to the curve
  that offers
  its weight
  as an anchor
  but you must remain agile
  yet responsive
  to every cross-current of wind.
  Don't worry so much about

learning all the names
of all the birds
just remember when & where they appear
so you can return later
& insert page breaks, or asterisks, or fall-out shelters
or lit candles –

you must hold in place
the many variables.
You must place yourself
at times detached
in closer relation.

Raccoons were roosting
in what you think is a Pecan tree.

But that was last year.
This year, this summer, this June, this June 30th
I find the absent crook
where the raccoons had been
& write them back in. I sit watching
for some landmark, new & of this June.
Any small signifier to distinguish
this present tense from all the rest
where I invent myself thusly –

it is a simultaneous event
in fast & slow motion
the whole song bag. A mosaic of cells.

I am guilty of clinging to this –

I wander out to the lobby & try to drink from the water
fountain but can't gauge the depth & get water up my nose.

I am guilty of that.
As if my purpose is as plain
as painting over cracks in the walls. As if my person is a collection of
gears
I roll out on the street each morning. A jumble of bees & straw men I
concoct to interface with the flowers & emails that make up the world.

While the fly-wheel in my chest bumps & whirs

I break from
the cadence & the round vowels
that plague it
because if you let the birds
wake you
you often find a brick
where the mind was
& when you return to the breath
you often find
you're not breathing at all.

HALFALOGUE

I'd socked myself into the shape of June & then as I watched the flame turn its counter-clockwork drum I woke as July widened. I wanted to write straight through it

as an arrow would. But the updrafts of the closer cliffs & the opposite push of the inward surging sea stirred it upward & out

while echoing back in, if that's possible –

I could say I built a boat. I could say I built a sky above & waves below. I could say I crossed large bodies of water, week after week with no land in sight.

I could say that I was at a party & a group was discussing a movie where the goal or the mission of the story was to 'get to the coast'. And someone asked why that was so common. Getting to the coast. And someone else asked if it was a biblical reference.

I could say I knew the answer but I couldn't say it. Because all I could come up with was, Wouldn't you? Given the time & freedom. Wouldn't you? And that's a line of a Jon Davis poem I coveted in my twenties & didn't realize I'd memorized until it appeared on my tongue like a ring does masquerading as my own.

I could say if the land was all a burned out narrative as far as the eye
could see
wouldn't you walk & walk, if you knew
there was another kind of surface

that curls toward you & back from you
as if beckoning & saying go! incessantly
while the rhythm crashes into its own arc?

I could say I was describing the draw of the ocean
but I'm confused about what is happening in this picture. As it was

overheard

& the chef was doing a French accent to justify something 'iconic'
that culminated in 'white beef stock'. That was the image given to
illustrate the point.

There was a desire for a set protocol. Someone suggested Peter & the
Wolf as a soundtrack. Someone else said, just the bassoons.

I wasn't talking to myself I was whispering. The computer kept
capitalizing my I. It just doesn't seem right to assume so much. This
was the slowest day of the year & I'm pretty sure it was miserable.

Or was I out of step with the font?
Or the convergence?

Or did I mean correspondence?

Someone left me a message at noon. It is long & very strange. At first

I thought it was someone eating an apple. But now I think it is horses
walking.

These aren't memories they are happenings.
They are happening. Smaller icebergs breaking off,
that can only be called small when compared to what they broke from.

To call all the small things. One ringy-dingy. Two ringy-dingy.

But we are past falling down. And past the hard work of it.

And so we weave it in with the hairs of your beard
& the YouTube video of a black phoebe doing nothing
other than screeching & cocking its slight head
to fix its glinting yellow eye on what seems to be us

watching it

over & over until it's grown dark
& just before sleep we realize
we forgot to flip the mattress again.
Or meaning to brush your teeth all morning.
I've been meaning to brush my teeth all morning.
Or meaning to donate blood. Or volunteer at a retirement home.
Or call Jenya, whose mother is dying.

Chris Daniels wrote: this bird lives us
& I want to agree
but our feet & tired-asses keep getting in the way of this.
I itch. I lick. I suck. I hunger. I sleep. I sup. I dither.

How Nora said she read an article about why overhearing a cell phone conversation is so annoying:

> *Researchers discovered that it takes more effort for the brain to understand only half a conversation or a "halfalogue" compared with a full dialogue between two people.*
>
> *"It's unbelievably irritating to overhear someone on a cell phone," said Lauren Emberson, the study co-author. "It's harder to tune out, you can't pull your attention away from it and you're more distracted by it.*

And how the same must be true with the image of a circle and its sound. I've begun to think my insistence on the bell, on the ringing of bells, on the rung bell & its ring was my inability to complete it.

From the glint
off the side
of its sleight of hand

a waterway opens where none had been prior
but pulls my boots off if I sink too long in it.

Even the quote I'd tacked above my desk: The soul is the prison of the body. We try to define to each other & yet we keep reversing which trait belonged to which & it's like rolling a kayak, when you roll over & over until you're no longer sure if you're above or below the water. Is now or now or now the time to breathe? I sighed, it requires so much of us doesn't it? And it was obvious neither of us knew if I meant the soul or the body.

And having woven my way into a labyrinth of my own making it seems appropriate to find at its center not a minotaur but a dog. A poodle exactly. Circling 3, 4, times. Because that's what you do. We do this. Sniff the spot. Round & round. We do this again & again. And fall asleep before ever starting or ending the poem.

WAR FLOWER

             The momentary throat
of evening

         lit lastly   the hills

scoured
of their wolves.

Touched back
from within,

what time could it have been?
It was probably five o'clock.

They must have run.
They must have.

Started by a wasp fright they must have
tightened toward a core in a frenzy

& seen the vertigo   counterpoint to the void
in the zoned off erosion.

This isn't that but a representative graph

to plot the words for things
twice-removed from the concussives

not the fish.

I'm no one's darling.
And you smell like a purple iris.

And the sudden is

an indentation
of damp circles   where the day will be
encapsulated & yet

blown open
to litter the hours
& readily take on
a howl

waking out of the rules
                    to find cats
                    had shit in the sandbox

        we pledge allegiance

                (They are a generation disinclined to song

with our crumpled hats
clenched to our sternums.

They must have run
roughshod, run over by wind

toward all the possible far-flung futures
born of the rows' exact cultivation

I may or may not
have seen you in

      as I have spent   as I AM spent,

leeched
& left fallow as a darker reflection

of the darkly rendered
           arrangement

touches back
a familial cadence,

the belligerence of snapping turtles
camouflaged among clots of algae   & the placid surface

     reflecting each leafless reach skyward
making out the edges

of their shells amidst the muddy bottom.

        Where a bird must have perched
among branches to bookmark this –

Pond where the train tracks run
toward their end

as slats of light tangle back

     siphoned toward the source

across the rumpled forest floor

they must have run

without knowing,
crossed over

without taking part.

What time could it have been?
It was probably war o'clock.

DEARS OF INTERNMENT

If distance is palpable

with pockets where tempo arrests,

unfix to particulars.
Select-all.
                        All of it.

If the sentence (my sentence
is a small diagram
of the larger system

                        at this moment
I feel very much
in the shadow of the moon

& find my eyes
adjunct to the splaying
where auto-shapes
reach some final velocity

                        & the prologue ringing is a flock of geese

galvanized, by proxy.

And although music is the most basic vehicle
used to facilitate escape

I find I can no longer move

tacked down by a basic sneeze
& other vertical strivings.

It is true I desire
not absence
          but to arrive after

where objects disappear
through overexposure.

          I mean, how I paraphrase
and take you out.

Meanwhile, at my father's bedside
I see the dead
begin to dream
him more clearly

          & counting out beats
where the same
self repeats

in the overlap
we thought

he was breathing
but it was just the machine.

The prerequisite accomplishment

of cells dying, dead. Cells dividing,
summoned, slight

        garrulous & socked-in it wasn't –

jumbled by foresight
this anniversary
ends
this anniversary

& starts a new meaning
please save
or
save now

where I mourn
the disappearance of the card catalogues
& the micro-fiche.

Or now, where there are so many animals.

In the voice

we are full
of their liturgy –

a plug that holds the presence in place.

Can space open up
& also be framed?

Because we sat
for a long while like that
in the car
in the parking lot
listening to the radio
static acted out

by the leafless boughs

& the owl familiar
the familiar bad luck

so you touch yourself
to find yourself
book-ended by bridges

trundled as asterisks
rise to the surface
& you do feel the roar –

the fossil
this one thought will become
contains less than 1%
of its meaning.

       A bird wing
where an eye should be.

A BIRD WING WHERE AN EYE SHOULD BE

NOTES

See also: http://bit.ly/12oRDC0

THE LONGEST TOTAL SOLAR ECLIPSE OF THE CENTURY
After lines from *The Blue Notebook* by Daniil Karmes
See also: http://bit.ly/YJJtf4

MUSICAL CHAIRS
Includes text from <u>The White Goddess</u> by Robert Graves and the
Wikipedia entry for The Pigeonhole Principle
See also: Lucas Samaras' painting *The Critics*

ZEITGEBERS
After Charles Wright's <u>Black Zodiac Poems</u>

ORCHESTRAL SCHEMATICS
"Plant corn when oak leaves are the size of a bat ear." Trini Campbell of
Riverdog Farm in Guinda, CA.
See also: http://bit.ly/YoxlDp

GEMINIDS
See also: http://bit.ly/YoC0VY

THE HUNG
Includes lines from an email from Chad Dean's dream

ESCAPE FROM THE LANGUAGE LAB
Includes a line from Jack Spicer's poem, *One Night Stand*

ALTERNATOR...
See also: Ansel Adams' photograph, *The Golden Gate,* San Francisco, 1933

AT IMPEDMENT
Includes lines from William Shakespeare's <u>Othello</u> & Robert Kelly's poem, *Arnaut Daniel*

CATHERINE MENG FINDS TENSES & PRONOUNS PAINFUL
See also: <u>This Compost</u> by Jed Rasula chapter, *The Floor is the Upside Down*

R.I.P. BABY HUMMINGBIRDS
Includes text from the Wikipedia entry for Estuaries, Jed Rasula's <u>This Compost</u> and Robert Pogue Harrison's, <u>Forests</u>
See also: http://bit.ly/YQ55J6

THIS POEM IS IN FOUR PARTS
Quotes Rae Armantrout reading at Studio One in Oakland, CA April 2010

GAME RESERVE
See also: *The Panther* by Rainer Maria Rilke

HALFALOGUE
See also: Jon Davis' poem, *The Hawk. The Road. The Sunlight After Clouds.*
See also: Chris Daniels' poem, *Corpografia*
Quotes <u>Discipline and Punish: The Birth of the Prison</u> by Michel Foucault

WARFLOWER
See also: Obi Kaufmann's collection of paintings by the same title

DEARS OF INTERNMENT
Includes text from *My Poetry Isn't Built on Hope* an interview with Rae Armantrout by Tom Beckett and text from <u>Notebooks of Malte Laurids Brigge</u> by Rainer Maria Rilke

ACKNOWLEDGEMENTS

Some of these poems have appeared in the following journals/web journals: *Aufgabe, Abraham Lincoln, Big Bell, Eleven Eleven, Horse Less Review, Omnidawn Poetry Feature, Salt Grass, Shampoo, TRY!*

Sincerest thanks to my friends, family, and SplitLevel Text for all of their support & assistance. A special thank you & supreme love to Elliot Fredericksen.

CATHERINE MENG

Catherine Meng is the author the chapbooks *15 Poems in Set of Five* (Anchorite Press), *Dokument* (Petrichord Books), *Lost Notebook w/ Letters to Deer* (Dusie3), and *I'm not writing PURE WAR this is a grocery list* (Dusie5), as well as a full-length poetry collection, *Tonight's the Night* (Apostrophe Books, 2007). Her poems have appeared in *Abraham Lincoln, Aufgabe, The Boston Review, Crowd, Fence, Jubilat,* and *Shampoo,* among other places. She lives in Berkeley, CA with her family.

SPLITLEVEL TITLES

Alan Gilbert, *The Treatment of Monuments*
Carla Harryman, *W—/M—*
Catherine Meng, *The Longest Total Solar Eclipse of the Century*
Jerome Rothenberg, *A Cruel Nirvana*

CPSIA information can be obtained at www.ICGtesting.com
Printed in the USA
BVOW02s0802260813

329287BV00003BA/21/P